Ooey-gooey Animals

Newts

Lola Schaefer

www.raintreepublishers.co.uk

Visit our website to find out more information about **Raintree** books.

To order:
☎ Phone 44 (0) 1865 888112
🖹 Send a fax to 44 (0) 1865 314091
💻 Visit the Raintree Bookshop at www.raintreepublishers.co.uk to browse our catalogue and order online.

First published in Great Britain by Raintree, Halley Court, Jordan Hill, Oxford OX2 8EJ, part of Harcourt Education.
Raintree is a registered trademark of Harcourt Education Ltd.

Editorial: Nick Hunter and Diyan Leake
Design: Sue Emerson (HL-US) and Joanna Sapwell
Picture Research: Amor Montes de Oca (HL-US) and Ginny Stroud-Lewis
Production: Lorraine Hicks

Originated by Dot Gradations
Printed and bound in China by South China Printing Company

ISBN 1 844 21023 5
07 06 05 04 03
10 9 8 7 6 5 4 3 2 1

British Library Cataloguing in Publication Data
Schaefer, Lola
Newts
597.8'5
A full catalogue record for this book is available from the British Library.

Acknowledgements
The publishers would like to thank the following for permission to reproduce photographs: Animals Animals p. **18** (Ted Levin); Ann & Rob Simpson p. **11**; Bruce Coleman Inc. p. **17** (R. Tercafs/TERCA); Color Pic, Inc. pp. **6** (E. R. Degginger), **9** (E. R. Degginger); Corbis pp. **5** (Joe McDonald), **10** (Kennan Ward), **13** (George McCarthy), **15** (Raymond Gehman), **16** (Lynda Richardson), **23** (mucus, Joe McDonald; tadpoles); Dan Suzio pp. **20**, **21**, **23** (larvae), back cover (larvae); David Liebman p. **19**; Denis Sheridan p. **23** (vertebrate); Dwight Kuhn pp. **1**, **4**, **8**, **14**, **22**, **24**, back cover (foot); Rick Wetherbee p. **7**; Visuals Unlimited p. **12** (Rob Simpson)

Cover photograph of a newt, reproduced with permission of Dwight Kuhn

Every effort has been made to contact copyright holders of any material reproduced in this book. Any omissions will be rectified in subsequent printings if notice is given to the publishers.

CAUTION: Remind children that it is not a good idea to handle wild animals. Children should wash their hands with soap and water after they touch any animal.

Some words are shown in bold, **like this.** You can find them in the glossary on page 23.

Contents

What are newts?

Newts are little animals that live in water.

They have a backbone, so they are **vertebrates**.

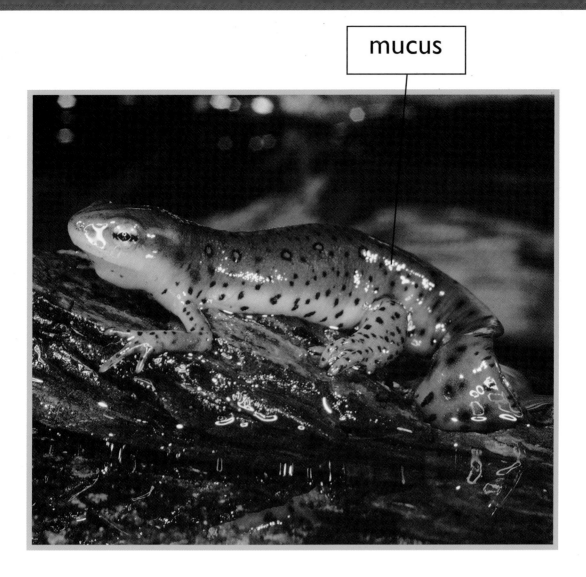

mucus

Newts have smooth skin.

They have **mucus** which keeps their skin wet.

Where do newts live?

Most newts live in streams or ponds.

Some kinds of newts live on land, part of the time.

Newts rest in the mud or on plants underwater.

What do newts look like?

Newts look like small lizards.

They have a thin body and a long tail.

tail

body

Most newts are brightly coloured.

What do newts feel like?

Newts feel sticky because of the **mucus** on their skin.

The mucus on many newts is a poison.

This poison stops bigger animals, like this heron, from eating them.

How big are newts?

Most newts can fit in your hand.

This is a small newt.

Some newts are as long as a pencil.

This is a big newt.

How do newts move?

Newts can walk.

They move one foot at a time.

Newts can swim.

They wiggle their body and tail to move through the water.

What do newts eat?

On land, newts eat slugs and worms.

They eat snails and insects, too.

In water, newts eat **tadpoles** and fish.

Newts catch food with their fast tongue.

What do newts do when it is cold?

Newts rest through the cold winter.

They need to keep warm.

Newts wiggle into small cracks in the ground or under logs.

They come out in warm weather.

Where do new newts come from?

larvae

Adult newts lay many eggs in water.

Larvae come out of the eggs.

legs

The larvae grow legs.

The little larvae grow into newts that can walk or swim.

Quiz

What are these newt parts?

Can you find them in the book?

Look for the answers on page 24.

?

?

?

Glossary

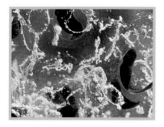

larvae
name for some animals when they have just come out of their egg

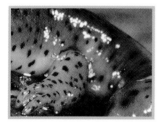

mucus
slimy stuff that animals have in or on their body

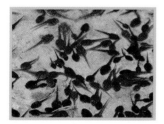

tadpoles
frog larvae

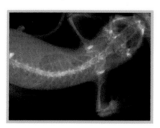

vertebrate
animal that has a backbone

Index

Answers to quiz on page 22

body

tail

leg

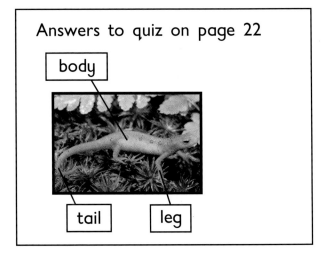

Titles in the Ooey-gooey Animals series include:

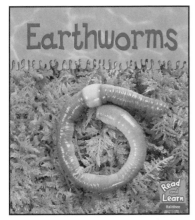

Hardback   1 844 21020 0

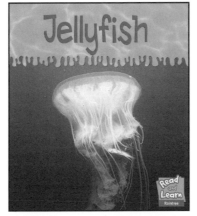

Hardback   1 844 21021 9

Hardback   1 844 21022 7

Hardback   1 844 21023 5

Hardback   1 844 21024 3

Hardback   1 844 21025 1

Hardback   1 844 21026 X

Find out about the other titles in this series on our website www.raintreepublishers.co.uk

Contents

Any words appearing in the text in bold, **like this**, are explained in the glossary. You can also look out for them in the Word bank at the bottom of each page.

Nasty and ghastly

You wake up in the morning and try to get out of bed. You feel terrible. You've got a sore throat and your head hurts. Your face is covered in spots. What do you do?

- You might crawl back into bed and hope to sleep it off.
- You might take some medicine.
- You might call the doctor.

The chances are it is nothing serious and you will soon feel better. But not so long ago you would be in a real panic. Being ill could be very nasty. Some of the treatments were also pretty nasty! For many people, feeling ill could mean death was on its way. . .

Tricky times

Growing up has always been a risky business. For centuries, one of the big risks to children has been disease. In the United States 150 years ago, only eight out of ten babies made it to their fifth birthday. Good health care today means over 99 percent of children survive.

Babies that are born today are much more likely to survive into adulthood.

Word bank   **rectum**   end part of the large intestine from which waste leaves the body

Nasty Bugs
and
Ghastly Medicine

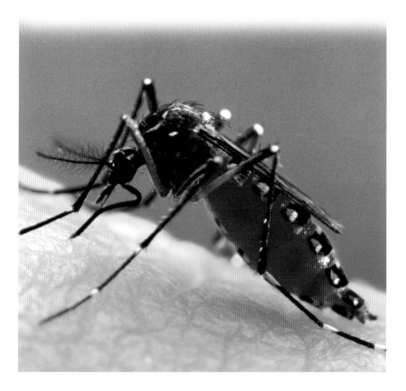

John Townsend

www.raintreepublishers.co.uk

Visit our website to find out more information about **Raintree** books.

To order:

☎ Phone 44 (0) 1865 888112

▤ Send a fax to 44 (0) 1865 314091

▭ Visit the Raintree Bookshop at www.raintreepublishers.co.uk to browse our catalogue and order online.

First published in Great Britain by Raintree, Halley Court, Jordan Hill, Oxford OX2 8EJ, part of Harcourt Education.
Raintree is a registered trademark of Harcourt Education Ltd.

Editorial: Melanie Waldron and Lucy Beevor
Design: Philippa Jenkins and Q2A
Illustrations: Q2A
Picture Research: Mica Brancic and Elaine Willis
Production: Chloe Bloom
Originated by Modern Age
Printed and bound in China by South China Printing Company

10 digit ISBN 1 406 20075 1
13 digit ISBN 978 1 406 20075 1

10 09 08 07 06
10 9 8 7 6 5 4 3 2 1

British Library Cataloguing in Publication Data
Townsend, John
Nasty bugs and ghastly medicine. –
(A painful history of childhood)
362.1'9892'0009
A full catalogue record for this book is available from the British Library.

Acknowledgements
Alamy pp. 20 (Brand X Pictures), 42–43 (Fotofacade), 32 (Jacky Chapman), 12–13 (Mike Stone), 40 (Steve Skjold), 22 (Terry Smith Images); Bridgeman Art Library p. 10; Bruce Coleman pp. 10–11; Corbis p. 36; Corbis pp. 5, 13, 14, 37 (Bettman), 8–9 (Brian F. Peterson), 4 (Cameron), 7 (Charles Mauzy), 4–5 (Gallo Images/Anthony Bannister), 16–17 (Lester V. Bergman), 18 (PHIL/CDC), 24 (Randy Faris), 6–7 (Reuters/Issei Kato); Empics p. 33 (AP); Getty Images pp. 20 (Abid Hatib), 32–33 (AFP), 41 (DATA/J. Tayloe Emery), 5(b), 14, 27, 34–35, 36–37 (Hulton Archive), 22 (Hulton Archive/ Fred Morely), 27 (National Geographic), 15 (PhotoDisc; PhotoLibrary.com), title and 38–39 (Stone); Getty Images News pp. 35, 43; Getty Images News p. 42 (Justin Sullivan); Mary Evans Picture Library pp. 18–19; Panos pp. 40–41 (Pep Bonet); Reuters p. 38; Rex pp. 5(m), 34 (Image Source), 25 (Phanie/Alix), 5(t), 12 (Sarah Flanagan); SPL/BSIP pp. 17 (Chassenet), 24, 28 (Studio), 29 (David Scharf), 30–31 (Dr John Brackenbury), 21 (Dr P. Marazzi), 19 (Jean-Loup Charmet), 8 (Paseika); TopFoto p. 23; Wellcome pp. 11, 26, 30.

Cover photograph of a nurse from the Mobile Voluntary Aid Detachment (VAD) giving a boy a dose of medicine, 1939, reproduced with permission of Getty/Hulton Archive.

The publishers would like to thank Bill Marriott for his assistance in the preparation of this book.

The nastier, the better!

Many diseases that can now be cured with medicines were killers over 100 years ago. New medicines, cleaner water, and healthier food have made growing up less risky than it used to be in many countries.

At one time a sick child could be given all sorts of terrible treatments. Many were also useless. How would you fancy these treatments?

- Having cuts made in your skin to bleed away the sickness.
- Having to eat vile mixtures and disgusting brews.
- Having mixtures pumped up the **rectum**.

An old belief was: "If it doesn't hurt, it doesn't work."

Leeches suck blood, and have been used to treat wounds for thousands of years.

Find out later

Why were children made to chew garlic?

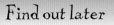

How were cows thought to help TB?

Why were children made to swallow cod liver oil?

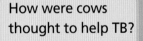

Old diseases, old cures

Roman babies

When a baby was born in ancient Rome, it would be placed at its father's feet. He would only pick it up and accept it if it looked healthy. If the baby looked sick or disabled, the father would turn away. The baby would be taken outside and left to die.

Thousands of years ago, giving birth was a great risk to both mother and baby. Disease could soon attack their bodies. In ancient Egypt, babies were lucky to be born safely and survive to their first birthday. Parents could only chant spells over their children in the hope of protecting them from illness.

Most parents used to have as many babies as possible. This was because many of the babies would die in their first few years. Only some would survive to become adults. The surviving children would go out to work and would also look after the parents in old age. So it was important to make sure families were large.

The carp fish is a symbol of strength and good health in Japan. ⋯⋗

Word bank   **asthma**   condition that causes difficulty in breathing, with wheezing and coughing

Healthy ideas

Many people hate eating cabbage. But this vegetable has been used in medicine for thousands of years. In ancient Rome raw cabbage was thought to cure many illnesses. In ancient China many other plants were used to cure illness. Herbs were hung up around houses, as people believed that they kept childhood diseases away.

In a similar way, kites in the shape of carp fish were hung up in Japanese homes. By doing this, parents hoped that the boy of the house would grow to be as healthy as the carp. Even now many Japanese families still celebrate the health of their children every year on *Kodomo-no-hi*, which means Children's Day.

Ancient treatment

Some Native Americans used the foul-smelling skunk cabbage (above) to treat childhood diseases. For centuries they used the **shoots** of the vegetable, which are poisonous until cooked. A mixture made from these was used to treat **whooping cough** and **asthma**.

whooping cough childhood disease that causes bad coughing attacks and loud gasping for breath

The Middle Ages

For most people who lived a thousand years ago in Europe, medical care was limited to healers, witch doctors, or the local "wise woman". These would offer lucky charms or mixtures made from parts of animals and plants. Some people thought a child with a fever or fits had evil spirits inside them. They thought spells or prayers were the only cure.

Some simple drugs were made from plants such as thyme, dandelion, or lavender. But these had little effect on many diseases. There was often little hope of a cure.

Special Ultraviolet (UV) lights show up bacteria on this hand.

Word bank   **bacteria**   very tiny living things, which can cause disease and infection

Filthy habits

People long ago knew nothing about **hygiene**. Children were not taught to wash their hands before eating or after going to the toilet. People living in the countryside shared their homes with animals. That meant lice and **ticks**, as well as dung and flies, were in the rooms where people lived.

Food was often left around for flies to crawl over, or was prepared with dirty hands. People ate with their fingers, often sharing bowls. They easily picked up bad **bacteria**, because they did not wash their hands or use spoons. No wonder people often became ill.

Eating and drinking with grubby hands spreads harmful bacteria.

hygiene   standards of keeping clean
tick   small bloodsucking animal that carries diseases

The Black Death

Across Europe in the 1300s one-third of all people died from what was called the "Black Death". Many children were among the 25 million people or so who died. In fact, in England in the 1360s, so many young people died that it was called the "**Plague** of Children".

Victims of the plague had fever, headaches, and swellings in the armpits. Within a week their skin often turned dark purple before they died. This is where the name "Black Death" came from. No one knew that it was caused by a **bacteria** carried by rat-fleas, and sometimes other rodents.

Plague victims were covered in terrible sores. ✝

Plague

Thousands of people died each week in Europe in the 1300s. Dead bodies littered the streets. As soon as a member of the family fell ill with the dreaded plague, children were sent away in case they also caught it. They would have to roam the streets in search of food . . . among the rotting bodies.

flu   short for influenza, a very infectious viral disease

Ghastly medicine

People tried all kinds of ways to treat the plague. None of these would have done any good at all:

- bathing in human urine
- rubbing dung over the skin
- placing dead animals in their homes
- putting leeches on the skin
- wearing a magpie's beak around the neck
- holding a live chicken on their swellings
- drinking a glass of urine twice a day.

Thousands of rats like these carried the plague bacteria all over Europe.

Costumes like this were worn by doctors to protect them against the plague.

Young and old alike

The Black Death began like **flu**. Victims had headaches, aching joints, fever, vomiting, and weakness. Fleas also spread the plague to dogs, cats, chickens, cows, donkeys, and sheep, which also died quickly.

11

You are what you eat

Garlic

Young people were often made to chew raw garlic to cure illness.

"Garlic kills worms in children, **purges** the head, is a cure for any **plague**, and takes away skin spots."

- Nicholas Culpeper, 1653, author of The English Physician

Garlic is now known to have many health benefits.

Garlic can help to get rid of a bad cold.

Many people had very little to eat 500 years ago. The food that they did have was not very **nutritious**. Children's growing bodies usually suffered the most.

Even rich children did not always have strong bones and teeth. People did not know the importance of brushing their teeth each day to get rid of **bacteria** in the mouth. Their teeth often decayed and gave them painful toothache. Some people in the **Middle Ages** believed toothache was caused by a worm in the tooth. There was even a "cure" for this: "Take a candle and burn it close to the tooth. The worms that are gnawing the tooth will fall out into a cup of water held by the mouth."

Word bank   **fungus**   plant-like living thing that feeds on material and makes it rot

In Europe, many of the women thought to be witches were drowned.

Food poisoning

We now know that eating rotting food can make us ill. In the Middle Ages, many people ate **rye** bread, but they did not know it was making them ill. **Fungus** called ergot could grow on rye and poison the bread. People who ate it rolled around in agony, with terrible burning pains. Children ran screaming into the streets and were thought to be mad.

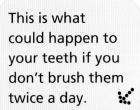

This is what could happen to your teeth if you don't brush them twice a day.

The illness was called St Anthony's Fire. It could not be treated. Victims felt like they were being burned alive. Blood did not flow to their fingers, toes, hands, or feet, so they dropped off with **gangrene**. Many children died from this poisoning.

Screaming teens

In Europe and North America in the 1600s, many young people were thought to be witches. That was because they often acted strangely and screamed a lot. In some cases this odd behaviour was probably caused by eating bread made from poisoned rye flour. This gave them the illness St Anthony's Fire.

nutritious   when a food is healthy and good for you
purge   clean out and make pure

Poor diet

Today we know that our bodies need different sorts of food and **vitamins** to stay healthy. Children who do not eat well do not grow properly and can develop illnesses. One common illness that affected young people throughout history was called rickets.

Rickets is a bone disease that affects young people who do not eat enough vitamin D or get enough sunlight on their bodies. Their bones go soft and weak. This can make their legs bend under weight, making walking very difficult. Historians think that around half of all poor children around the world in the 1600s suffered from rickets.

Cod liver oil

Cod liver oil tastes horrible, but many people believe it does you good! For hundreds of years, children were given spoonfuls of cod liver oil (above). Many still are, but **capsules** now make it easier to swallow. Cod liver oil is rich in vitamin D and can sometimes stop children from getting rickets.

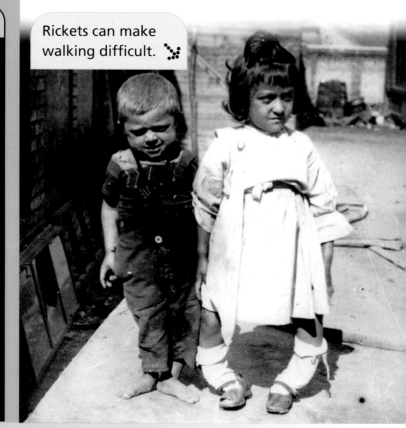

Rickets can make walking difficult.

Word bank   **beriberi**   disease caused by a poor diet, making people's bodies weak

Healthy eating

In the 1650s an English doctor, called Francis Glisson, noticed that many young people had gum disease, loose teeth, and fever. They had a disease called scurvy.

Sailors could also get scurvy. They were at sea for many months, and they only ate the food that had been brought onto the ship. This did not include fruit, which contains vitamin C. A lack of vitamin C causes scurvy. Many young people were also not eating enough fruit, and without vitamin C, they were developing scurvy.

Vitamin B is found in whole cereals, bread, eggs, green vegetables, cheese, and nuts. People who did not eat enough vitamin B or B_1 could also become weak and ill, and some would get a disease called **beriberi**. This can be cured with a healthy diet.

Get to sleep!

Parents used all kinds of ways to get their sick children to sleep:

- **Opium** added to wine would put them to sleep, but too much stopped them waking up!
- Eating nettles mixed with the white of an egg was meant to help sleep.
- Stuffing a mattress with oats was thought to help a good night's sleep.

How would you like to eat nettles mixed with the white of an egg before bedtime?

vitamins   chemicals needed in small amounts in our food to keep us healthy

Diseases and vaccines

Some diseases often strike young people more than adults. This might be because young people have less **resistance** to some disease. Some major childhood diseases have killed many and affected millions.

Chickenpox

One of the most common **infectious** childhood diseases is chickenpox. It is very itchy because the chickenpox **virus** leaves the skin with hundreds of **pus**-filled blisters. These burst and form scabs. There is now a **vaccine** for chickenpox, which means that the disease may be wiped out in the future.

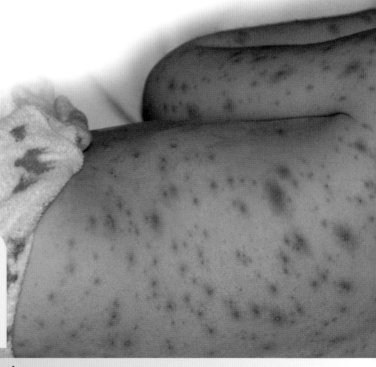

Today, children who get chickenpox usually have very itchy skin for about a week. •••⟩

immune able to resist an infectious disease because of a previous attack or a vaccination

Not too nasty

The only lasting effect of chickenpox is a few tiny scars left from the blisters that covered the skin. Blisters can even appear in the mouth and on the eyelids. In most cases today, healthy children soon recover as their bodies can fight the illness. Then they are usually **immune** to the disease and never catch it again. Chickenpox is serious only in rare cases. Even so, almost 10,000 Americans go to hospital with chickenpox each year. Most of these are adults, as the disease can be much worse the older a person gets.

Why chickenpox?

How did chickenpox get its name? Which of these is true?

- The specks that appear on the skin look as though they have been pecked by chickens.
- The skin and scabs look like chick peas.
- The disease was "nothing serious" so it was just a "chicken" version of the pox.

Look on page 44 for the answer.

Do chickenpox scabs look like chickpeas?

resistance   being able to fight back and stop something happening

17

Smallpox

If a child in the 1700s got itchy spots and felt unwell, there was panic. The illness might only have been chickenpox. On the other hand, it could have been the start of something far worse . . . the dreaded **smallpox**. This disease killed about one-third of the children who caught it. Those who survived could be left blind or scarred with **pockmarks**.

Smallpox is a **virus** that spreads through direct contact and on bedding or clothes. But in ancient China, people found a way to stop people from catching this disease. They blew dust from dried smallpox scabs into peoples' noses, which acted as a sort of **vaccination** against the disease.

Word bank   **smallpox** highly infectious dangerous disease causing blisters all over the body

Breakthrough

Edward Jenner was an English doctor. He knew that milkmaids often caught a weak form of smallpox from cows, called cowpox. But they never caught real smallpox. Why? Did the cowpox protect them?

In May 1796 Jenner tested out an idea on his gardener's son, eight-year-old James Phipps. He injected James with **pus** from a milkmaid's cowpox blister. James became slightly ill over the next nine days, but on the tenth day he was feeling better. On 1 July Jenner injected James with smallpox. It was a big risk, but smallpox did not develop. James was the first known boy to be **vaccinated** against smallpox. It was a major discovery.

Edward Jenner's clever discovery has saved thousands of lives over hundreds of years.

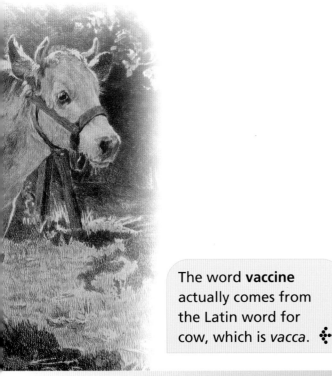

The word **vaccine** actually comes from the Latin word for cow, which is *vacca*.

Lives saved

It took a long time before Edward Jenner's vaccine prevented everyone from catching smallpox. Making enough vaccine and getting it around the world took doctors almost 200 years! At last, in 1980, smallpox became the first human disease to be wiped out throughout the world.

---

vaccinate inject a patient with medicine that makes the body fight a disease

MMR

A vaccine called MMR is given to babies in over 100 different countries, including the United States, Australia, New Zealand, and most countries in Europe. This vaccine is for measles, mumps, and **rubella**. More than 500 million MMR **doses** have been given worldwide in the last 30 years.

Measles

Measles is a very common disease that has affected millions of young people over thousands of years. It spreads through sneezing, and starts with a sore throat, runny nose, and fever. Then an itchy rash appears on the skin. Although measles only lasts for about a week if a healthy person gets it, it can be a nasty disease for anyone with no **resistance.**

There are 30 million cases of measles each year, and over 1 million deaths. Most of these are in Africa. **Vaccines** have been used for just over 40 years but many people in poor countries cannot afford them.

A baby receives an MMR jab. 🔎

Measles can give a patient a red and itchy rash. 🔎

Word bank   epidemic   outbreak of disease that spreads quickly over a wide area

The 1800s

Measles can spread quickly. There were many **epidemics** in the 1800s that killed children, and millions of adults were also affected.

- In 1846 measles swept through the Faroe Islands near Iceland. Nearly 80 percent of the population caught the disease.
- In the mid-1800s, many Native Americans in North America died from measles because they had never come into contact with it before. This meant they had not built up any resistance. They caught the disease from Europeans who settled across the country.
- During the American Civil War (1861–1865), there were measles epidemics among the 4 million soldiers. About 100,000 men caught the disease, with almost 3,000 dying from it.

Can you believe it?

Before measles vaccines were first used in the 1960s, some mothers would hold "measles parties". If their child got measles they asked other parents living nearby to rush their children over. By playing with the **infected** child, other children caught the disease and got it over with while they were still young. In the United Kingdom, measles parties are now making a comeback amongst those parents who are against the MMR vaccine.

Koplik spots are small, white spots that appear on the inside of the cheeks during measles.

rubella mild infectious disease, also known as German measles

Gross treatments

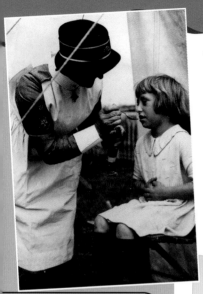

Throughout history, sick children have had to swallow all kinds of homemade mixtures in the belief that these would make them better. Sometimes the mixtures were spread over their bodies.

Worth a try?

These are just a few old "cures" from around 100 years ago in the United States:

- To cure chickenpox, go to a henhouse at night and let a black chicken fly over you.

- The roots of rhubarb hung around the neck will stop stomach aches.

- If a big red onion is tied to a bedpost whoever sleeps in the bed will not catch a cold.

- A dirty sock worn around the neck when you go to bed will cure a sore throat.

– Peggy Fisher, West Virginia Historical Society.

Ghastly castor oil

The castor bean plant grows in Africa. Its crushed seeds produce oil. The Egyptians chewed the seeds and swallowed them to relieve **constipation**. For hundreds of years, children have been made to swallow foul-tasting castor oil for the same reason (above). It can work very quickly. Sometimes it was just given to punish them!

Spreading grease on the skin was meant to cure a cold.

Word bank **constipation** difficulty going to the toilet to empty the bowel of waste

Mustard powder

Mustard seeds are known for their strong smell and spicy taste. For thousands of years mustard powder, made from crushed mustard seeds, was used in medicine. A mustard bath or rub was meant to cure everything from coughs and colds, to bedsores and snoring. Sick children often had to wear mustard plasters for bad coughs. Mustard paste was spread on a flannel and put on the chest. It would soon burn the skin and smell terrible.

A poster from the 1900s advertises a mustard footbath as a cure for a cold.

Gross grease

How would you like sheep fat to be rubbed on your chest and then to be wrapped in brown paper like a parcel? This treatment was used to treat colds in the United Kingdom around a hundred years ago. In parts of the United States mothers would put a hot cloth covered with sheep fat or goose grease on a sick child's chest to keep out the cold.

Ouch!

Ghastly medicine is bad enough when it tastes terrible. But having an injection can be even worse. The best place to jab a needle into a person is where they have most flesh – in the bottom! A **syringe** can be used to get some medicines into the body very quickly. This can often be better than swallowing them. If you inject a **dose** of medicine straight into a vein, it gets into the blood stream straight away. This means it can start fighting the disease immediately.

Getting the point

Two American businessmen met at a sales meeting in 1897. They made a deal and began a medical tools company: Becton, Dickinson, and Company. Their first new product was a brand new idea – an all-glass syringe that sold for just £1.40. Before long the syringe was selling all over the United States and saving many children's lives.

Injections can be scary, but they are over within a second.

The first syringes were very blunt.

Word bank   **disposable**   made to be thrown away after use
hypodermic   injected beneath the skin

Needles

At one time needles used for injections were large and used over and over again. This was dangerous and could spread disease, as well as making the needles blunt. The blunter they became, the more painful they were to the patient. Today needles are much sharper than they used to be.

In 1844 an Irish doctor, called Francis Rynd, invented the hollow needle. Next they needed to work out how to make a hollow needle thin enough and strong enough to pierce the skin, and to give just the right dose. Alexander Wood, a Scottish doctor, experimented with this idea and developed a new syringe that gave all these benefits. It was called the **hypodermic** needle, and is still in use in hospitals and surgeries today.

Disposable syringes are a much cleaner way to inject patients with medicine.

Millions of jabs

The first **mass-produced** syringes and needles were made and used from 1954. They were developed to give over 1 million US children the first ever **vaccine** for **polio**. These syringes and needles were **disposable**, so were used only once. This is much safer than re-using needles.

syringe   tool used to inject fluid into the body through a needle

Children's hospitals

Today's children's hospitals and young people's wards try to make a stay in hospital as pleasant and pain-free as possible. It was not always that way. In fact, young people were kept well away from hospitals for hundreds of years. They were not usually allowed inside.

It was only about 150 years ago that special hospitals began to be built just for the young. The first children's hospitals in the United States and the United Kingdom were built in the 1850s. At that time all hospitals were scary places because there were still no proper **anaesthetics**. Only very sick people went to hospital where often they died or caught even more disease.

In the 1800s many young people grew up in city **slums** where diseases spread quickly. With so many young people needing treatment, some cities began to build hospitals especially for them. The first was the Hospital for Sick Children at Great Ormond Street, London, UK, in 1852.

The first children's hospital in the United States was built in Philadelphia in 1855.

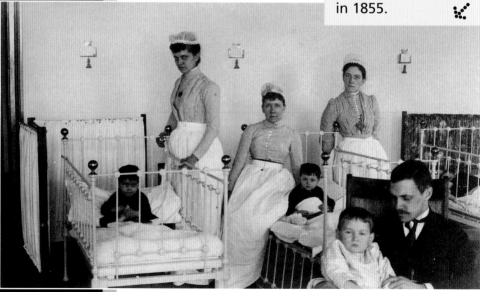

Word bank

anaesthetic drugs to make patients sleep, or treatment less painful

Not so child-friendly

Where there were no children's hospitals, very sick children were put in corners of adult wards or in cots in spare spaces. Here they were exposed to all kinds of other illnesses.

The first children's hospitals, like all other hospitals at the time, were run with strict rules. They had little to cheer up the patients and were not the welcoming places they try to be today. Parents were not able to visit their young children very often or to stay overnight.

A doctor and nurse examine a sick patient at a London children's hospital, 1870.

Lice like these lived in children's hair and clothes.

ringworm disease caused by fungus, that makes ring-shaped patches appear on the skin

Extreme treatment

In the late 1800s, some parents made sure their children went to the toilet every day to stay healthy. They were sure that a lot of bad health was caused by **constipation**, so all young people had to "keep their **bowels** moving". Stewed prunes, syrup of figs, or castor oil usually kept the bowels working regularly.

If these treatments did not work, it was time for an **enema**. A tube would be pushed into the child's bottom and warm soapy water was pumped up. Sometimes salts or other mixtures were added to help flush out the bowels.

Worms

At the end of the 1800s, many homes in the United States did not have drains to take away **sewage**. This meant diseases and **parasites** such as **hookworms** were everywhere. In the summer many children did not wear shoes. Young hookworms often got into children's bodies between their toes.

Feeling flushed

Children have been given enemas for thousands of years in the belief they cure all kinds of illnesses. They were used as long ago as ancient Greek and Chinese times. Native Americans also gave enemas, using hollow bones to pump the mixtures up into the bowels.

The dreaded enema kit.

Word bank   **bile**   thick, bitter, yellow-green fluid made by the liver
enema   liquid pumped into the bowels to clean them out

After making their way through the skin and into the body, the worms got to the intestine. They would live there, sucking the victim's blood for up to five years.

The first clinic for treating hookworm disease opened in 1910, in Columbia, Mississippi, United States. After taking a medicine to kill the worms inside the intestines, patients then had to have an enema to flush out the dead worms.

A painful end

In the United Kingdom in the 1800s, older children were sometimes given daily enemas of green soapsuds, ox **bile**, and other nasty mixtures. Some badly behaved young people were thought to need "cleansing" of their bad behaviour, so they were forced to have an enema.

This is a hookworm seen under a microscope. Imagine having hundreds of these in your stomach!

parasite insect or small animal which lives in or on another living thing

20th-century discoveries

Did you know?

Diphtheria comes from the Greek word *diphthera*, which means leather. This is because a leathery layer grows in the throat (below) of people with the disease. From 1735 to 1740, a diphtheria **epidemic** in New England, United States, killed almost 80 percent of children under ten years of age.

Within the last 100 years, medical science has made huge progress. Doctors now know how childhood diseases spread, and which drugs can treat them. Many countries now have cleaner water, healthier food, and better living conditions. In some parts of the world, many of the killer diseases of the past are no longer feared.

Diphtheria

Diphtheria was once one of the most common causes of death in children, usually where they were crowded together in dirty homes. But the disease is now rare in richer parts of the world where a **vaccine** has been used since the 1920s.

Big killer

Diphtheria starts like **flu**, with a fever and a sore throat. People catch it by breathing in diphtheria **bacteria** from droplets when an **infected** person coughs or sneezes. It can also be spread by touching used tissues, or by drinking from a glass used by an infected person. The disease causes breathing problems, heart failure, and sometimes death. Nearly one out of every ten children who catch diphtheria will die from it. In the early 1900s, in the United States, about 15,000 children and adults died every year from the disease. Now there are hardly any deaths from diphtheria.

Still lurking

An epidemic of diphtheria in Eastern Europe caused over 5,000 deaths between 1990 and 1995. In the United States, since 1980, there have been fewer than five cases reported each year.

When you sneeze, 2,000 to 5,000 bacteria-filled droplets are released into the air at a speed of 100 metres per second (0.06 miles per second)!

Whooping cough

Whooping cough is a highly **infectious** disease caused by **bacteria**. It can now be prevented with a **vaccine**. There are 30 to 50 million cases each year, and about 300,000 children under one year old still die from it. Older children, with stronger, more developed bodies usually survive the disease. In adults, the disease is usually very mild.

About 90 percent of all cases happen in poorer countries. Whooping cough lasts about six weeks, when the child finds it hard to sleep and eat. It starts like a cold and leads to a hacking cough with a "whoop" noise as the child tries to breathe.

Whooping cough causes a violent cough.

Word bank   tetanus   dangerous infectious disease causing stiffness, locking of the jaws, and often death

Saving lives

For hundreds of years, parents could do nothing to help children coughing all day and night. It took many years of study in the 1800s before doctors found out about different bacteria and how to deal with them. It was not until the 1920s that Dr. Louis Sauer developed a vaccine for whooping cough at Evanston Hospital, Illinois, United States. It took many more years to test the vaccine and make sure it was safe.

In the 1930s, in the United States, whooping cough killed about 6,000 children under the age of five every year. Making enough vaccine for millions of children took a long time, but by the 1950s mass vaccination was underway.

Baby jabs

Babies in richer countries are now given DTaP injections to protect them against diphtheria, whooping cough, and **tetanus**. Over 3 million US children now have the vaccine every year.

Injections are part of growing up for most babies today.

A child receives the whooping cough vaccine.

33

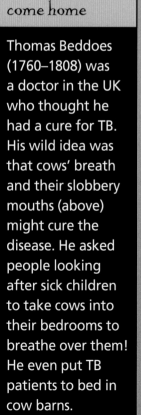

Tuberculosis

Tuberculosis (TB) was another deadly disease that spread quickly in crowded **slums**. In the 1800s TB killed more people in Europe and the United States than any other disease. About 90 percent of people in towns were **infected** with TB. Many of those were children.

Before drugs could treat the disease, doctors often put patients to bed outside! They believed plenty of fresh air was the answer. In winter, children would often lie in bed while snow fell on their pillow. With improvements to housing, plumbing, diets, and medical care throughout the 1900s, the number of TB cases dropped quickly.

Until the cows come home

Thomas Beddoes (1760–1808) was a doctor in the UK who thought he had a cure for TB. His wild idea was that cows' breath and their slobbery mouths (above) might cure the disease. He asked people looking after sick children to take cows into their bedrooms to breathe over them! He even put TB patients to bed in cow barns.

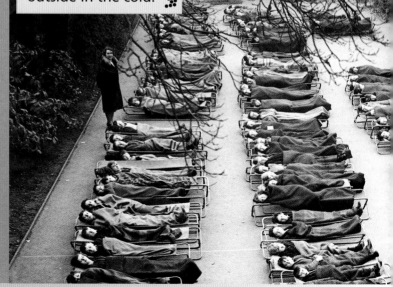

TB patients often felt worse after sleeping outside in the cold.

Word bank **antibiotic** drugs, such as penicillin, that can treat many diseases caused by bacteria or fungi

The big breakthrough in fighting TB came when Dr Alexander Fleming from Scotland found a way to kill harmful **bacteria** in the 1920s.

The first TB **vaccine** to be used on humans was made in 1921. In the 1940s and 1950s new **antibiotic** drugs could fight TB bacteria. By 1985, the number of deaths in the United States had fallen to the lowest figure ever recorded. Today most young people in richer countries are **vaccinated** against TB in high school.

In children and young people, TB causes:
- fever
- loss of weight
- sweating at night
- chills
- coughing up of blood.

21st century

TB is still around today. In the year 2003, there were 14,000 new cases of TB reported in the United States. In poorer countries, the disease still kills over 1 million people every year.

The cloudy areas on this X-ray show the TB damage to a patient's lungs.

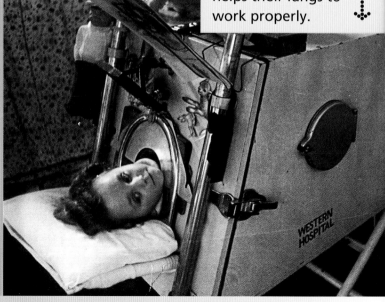

Polio

A cruel illness called **polio** has struck down young people all through history. They often caught it from infected water. It attacked their **nervous system** and often left them disabled for life. Polio brought misery to many homes in the first half of the 20th century.

Polio starts with a headache, fever, and stiffness in the body. The limbs can become **paralysed**. Sometimes breathing becomes so difficult that the victim dies from **suffocation**. One way of helping polio sufferers to breathe was to put them inside an iron lung. This was a machine with a pump inside.

Franklin D. Roosevelt in his wheelchair.

Famous victims

The Roman emperor Claudius who ruled from AD 41 to 54 caught polio as a child, which left him with one leg shorter than the other. His weak neck muscles made his head flop over, and he was left with speech problems. The former US president Franklin D. Roosevelt caught polio in 1921 at the age of 39, and was paralysed from the waist down.

The iron lung changes the air pressure around the patient, which helps their lungs to work properly.

Word bank   **nervous system**   network of nerves around the body that make different parts move

The war on polio

Polio **epidemics** affected the whole of the United States, from 1945 to 1949, with an average of over 20,000 cases a year. Two US scientists worked throughout the 1940s on a **vaccine** for polio. One, called Jonas Salk, finally tested his vaccine on monkeys in the 1950s. The first vaccine was used on children in 1952. The other scientist, Albert Sabin, kept working on the vaccine so that within 10 years it could be swallowed, rather than injected.

Mass vaccination against polio was done in Europe, Australia, and the United States in the 1960s. Soon children were safe from the dreaded **virus**. There were still some minor cases of polio in the 1980s, but the United States was polio-free by this time.

Great progress

- After 2001, 575 million children around the world were given the polio vaccine.
- After 2004, just over 1,000 cases of polio were reported in some poorer countries.
- By 2010 it is hoped that the world will be declared free of polio forever.

Many polio sufferers have to wear supports on their legs to help them walk.

paralysed   being unable to move
suffocation   being unable to breathe

Up to date

Young people can be saved from malaria today. The problem is getting the latest drugs to all the sufferers. More should be done to control the mosquitoes and more education is needed to teach children how to stop getting bitten. Bill Gates, the world's richest man, has given millions of dollars to help in the battle against malaria.

Many young people today are still at risk from disease in some parts of the world. Nasty bugs are always ready to strike.

Malaria is one disease that attacks children and adults in many hot countries. This dreaded illness has killed more people throughout history than any other. With one bite, a mosquito carrying malaria can pass tiny **parasites** into the bloodstream. This causes a fever like **flu**. It may damage the brain, make parts of the body fail, and even kill. There are at least 300 million cases of malaria each year. It is the main killer of African children under the age of five. Two children die of malaria every minute in Africa.

Bill Gates visits a baby girl in Africa, where he has helped to save many lives.

Meningitis

A disease that is still of concern to younger people in richer countries is meningitis.

- Meningitis strikes about 3,000 Americans each year, killing around 300 people. A similar number are affected in the United Kingdom.
- Cases among teenagers and young adults have more than doubled since 1991.
- Five to fifteen college students die each year in the United States from meningitis.

The early warning signs include:
- high fever
- neck stiffness
- rash
- bad headache
- a dislike of bright lights and sound.

The disease can be treated but it has to be caught quickly.

Today's world

Even in the 21st century, over 10 million children under the age of five die each year from diseases that can be prevented or treated. Two reasons are:

- Millions of the world's children still do not have enough to eat. They are too weak to fight disease.
- Poor countries cannot afford all the **vaccines** and medicines that are needed.

Despite its tiny size, the mosquito (enlarged here) is one of the most dangerous insects in the world.

HIV and AIDS

Many young people today have to face another threat. Millions of children carry the HIV **virus** that can develop into the disease called AIDS. Others have to look after parents who become ill from this virus. Millions of children have already lost their parents to AIDS in Africa alone.

Since it was first discovered in the late 1970s, HIV has spread all around the world. Millions of people go on to develop AIDS. Over 20 million have died so far. AIDS causes the **immune system** to fail so the body can no longer fight **infections** properly. There is still no known cure.

The international symbol for AIDS is a red ribbon.

21st century epidemic

It is thought that about five young people (between 10 and 24 years old) are infected with the HIV virus every minute somewhere in the world. Of the estimated 35 to 40 million people who have the HIV virus in their bodies, nearly 3 million are under 15 years old.

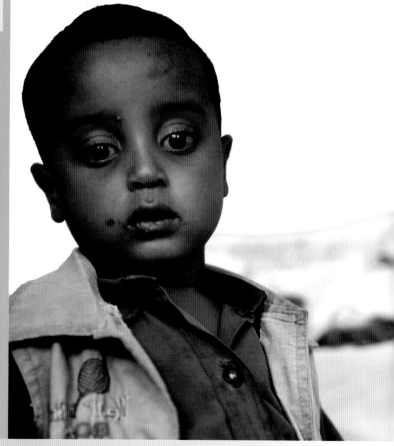

Word bank   carrier   someone who carries a virus or an infectious disease

Did you know?

Unlike other viruses, HIV is not passed from one person to another by sneezing and touching. The virus can only infect someone if a **carrier's** body fluid, such as blood, gets into his or her own body. Mothers with HIV can infect their unborn babies, so many children around the world are infected from birth.

People who inject drugs and share needles are at a greater risk of catching the HIV virus. Having unprotected sex can also spread the disease. Some drugs can slow down the effects of AIDS and can stop new viruses getting into the body. But these drugs cost a lot, and 95 percent of the people with HIV and AIDS live in poor countries.

Millions of young people across the world lose their parents to AIDS every day.

A growing problem

- Every year over 3 million people die of AIDS, including more than half a million children.
- Every year over 125,000 children in the United States become **orphans** because of AIDS.
- By 2010 around 40 million children round the world will be orphans because of AIDS.

The movie star Brad Pitt visits orphans living in an AIDS orphanage.

immune system body's natural system of fighting infection

41

Teens of tomorrow

One day we may get rid of the diseases that threaten today's young people. With more progress in medical science, more education, and work to prevent disease in poor countries, the future might be free from the fear of malaria and AIDS. After all, at one time, no one imagined that **smallpox** or **polio** could be wiped out forever.

In the past, **beriberi** and rickets were caused by poor food. Today the problem in rich countries is more often due to too much food. Childhood **obesity** is a growing health problem for many young people who eat too much fat and sugar, without getting enough exercise.

Keeping healthy

The health problems of young people in richer countries may have more to do with their unhealthy **environment**. Some diseases like **asthma** are growing, and this can be caused by **pollution**. Obesity can be another problem. Yet the best treatment for this is not "ghastly medicine", but just a healthy diet and plenty of exercise.

In 2005 Hurricane Katrina hit the United States. The storm left a trail of dangerous pollution and **sewage**, which could have led to a serious outbreak of disease.

Word bank | environment surroundings we live in
obesity very overweight

Healthy times?

Despite the problems of obesity, malaria, and AIDS there have never been so many healthy children on the planet! Of the world's 2 billion children and teenagers alive today, millions are very fit and healthy – more than ever before.

The good news is that so many of the nasty bugs and ghastly medicines of the past are now history. Not only have doctors made great progress in fighting diseases that once killed us, but we now know a lot more about **hygiene**, healthy eating, and exercise. Children who are able to keep clean, eat wisely, and keep fit now have a high chance of living long and healthy lives.

The task ahead

Every year, 2 million children under the age of five still die of diseases that are no longer a threat in rich countries. Measles, polio, **whooping cough**, TB, and diphtheria can all be prevented today with **vaccinations**. With more money and effort, such "nasty bugs" could be left behind forever.

Which girl is eating healthy food?

Happy and healthy!

Find out more

Answer from page 17…

How did chickenpox get its name? Any of the explanations from page 17 could be true! Chicken pox has nothing to do with chickens. Instead, the red spots were thought to look like chickpeas on the skin. The most likely explanation is that *varicella*, the Latin name for chickenpox, may have come from *cicer*, meaning chickpeas.

Further reading

A Painful History of Medicine: Pox, Pus & Plague, John Townsend (Raintree, 2005)

Great Inventions: Medicine, Paul Dowswell (Heinemann Library, 2001)

The Smallpox Slayer, Alan Brown (Hodder Children's Books, 2001)

Using the Internet

Explore the Internet to find out more about childhood medicine through time. You can use a search engine, such as **www.yahooligans.com**, and type in keywords such as:

● cod liver oil

● measles

● plague.

Search tips

There are billions of pages on the Internet so it can be difficult to find exactly what you are looking for.

These search tips will help you find useful websites more quickly:

● Know exactly what you want to find out about first.

● Use two to six keywords in a search, putting the most important words first.

● Be precise. Only use names of people, places, or things.

Timeline of vaccines for childhood disease

1796	First vaccine for smallpox, and the first vaccine for any disease.
1879	First vaccine for cholera.
1885	First vaccine for rabies.
1897	First vaccine for plague.
1921	First vaccine for TB.
1923	First vaccine for diphtheria.
1926	First vaccine for whooping cough.
1927	First vaccine for tetanus.
1945	First vaccine for influenza (flu).
1952	First vaccine for polio.
1954	First plastic disposable syringes for vaccines.
1962	First polio vaccine given by mouth.
1963	First vaccine for measles.
1967	First vaccine for mumps.
1970	First vaccine for rubella.
1970s	First vaccine for chickenpox.
1978	First vaccine for meningitis.

Glossary

anaesthetic drugs to make patients sleep, or treatment less painful

antibiotic drugs, such as penicillin, that can treat many diseases caused by bacteria or fungi

asthma condition that causes difficulty in breathing, with wheezing and coughing

bacteria very tiny living things, which can cause disease and infection

beriberi disease caused by a poor diet, making people's bodies weak

bile thick, bitter, yellow-green fluid made by the liver

bowels lower part of the intestine where waste is stored

capsule small pill with a shell that contains liquid medicine

carrier someone who carries a virus or an infectious disease

constipation difficulty going to the toilet to empty the bowel of waste

disposable made to be thrown away after use

dose measured amount of a medicine to be taken at one time

enema liquid pumped into the bowels to clean them out

environment surroundings we live in

epidemic outbreak of disease that spreads quickly over a wide area

flu short for influenza, a very infectious viral disease

fungus plant-like living thing that feeds on material and makes it rot

gangrene when flesh rots due to infection or poor blood supply

hookworm parasite worm with strong hooks to make it latch onto the intestine

hygiene standards of keeping clean

hypodermic injected beneath the skin

immune able to resist an infectious disease because of a previous attack or a vaccination

immune system body's natural system of fighting infection

infectious spreads easily from one person to another

mass produced many made at once, all exactly the same

Middle Ages period of European history from about AD 500 to 1500

nervous system network of nerves around the body that make different parts move

nutritious when a food is healthy and good for you

obesity very overweight

opium drug made from opium poppies, once used to help people sleep

orphan child whose parents have died

paralysed being unable to move

parasite insect or small animal which lives in or on another living thing

plague deadly disease that spreads quickly

pockmark round scar left on the skin after disease

polio infectious virus that causes children to lose the use of limbs

pollution unclean air or water

purge clean out and make pure

pus thick, foul-smelling liquid made by infected wounds

rectum end part of the large intestine from which waste leaves the body

resistance being able to fight back and stop something happening

ringworm disease caused by a fungus, that makes ring-shaped patches appear on the skin

rubella mild infectious disease, also known as German measles

rye cereal grass grown for grain or made into flour

sewage waste materials carried away by sewers

shoots young growth and new leaves of a plant

slum city area of dirty run-down housing, and poor living conditions

smallpox highly infectious dangerous disease causing blisters all over the body

suffocation being unable to breathe

syringe tool used to inject fluid into the body through a needle

tetanus dangerous infectious disease causing stiffness, locking of the jaws, and often death

tick small bloodsucking animal that carries diseases

vaccinate inject a patient with medicine that makes the body fight a disease

vaccine medicine to make the body defend itself against a disease

virus tiny living organism that breaks into the body's cells and can cause disease

vitamins chemicals needed in small amounts in our food to keep us healthy

whooping cough childhood disease that causes bad coughing attacks and loud gasping for breath

Index